POLITICIANS SAY THE DUMBEST THINGS

COLLECTED BY CAROL ROESSLER

(i)

Copyright © 1999 by Carol Roessler

All rights reserved. First edition 1999. No part of this book may be reproduced in any form without written permission from the publisher, Wright Strategies, P.O. Box 1614, Oshkosh, Wisconsin 54903 (877) 920-6889

Printed in the United States of America
Second printing June 2000

Library of Congress Cataloging-in-Publication Data:
Roessler, Carol.
Politicians Say The Dumbest Things
by Carol Roessler
Library of Congress Catalog Card Number: 98-61614
ISBN 0-9668446-0-2

Action Printing
N6637 Rolling Meadows Drive
Fond du Lac, Wisconsin 54937

Cover and book design by CI Design
Illustrations by Rodney Gile

Comments collected by listening, reading, observing and internet perusal.

Some quotes reprinted with permission from *Wit and Wisdom of Politics* by Chuck Henning. © 1996 Fulcrum Publishing, Inc., Golden, Colorado. All rights reserved.

POLITICIANS SAY THE DUMBEST THINGS

"Being in politics is like being a football coach: you have to be smart enough to understand the game and dumb enough to think it's important."

– *Eugene McCarthy*

"I hate to confuse myself
with the facts."

"These numbers are not my own, they are from someone who knows what he's talking about!"

"There is a 999 chance
out of 100 that I will
support this bill."

"There is nothing wrong with clean, pure cigar smoke."

"I was a third term
    freshman when you were
    a first term freshman."

"I know that he wants
to require everyone
to expose themselves
to everyone else."

"That's enough to make one's back leg stand up."

"As long as I am in the
Senate, there will not be
a nuclear waste suppository
in my district."

"This bill will help rural Wisconsin and sparsely populated big cities."

"People planning on getting in serious accidents should have their seat belts on."

"This is a good health care bill. Take it from one who has survived a terminal heart attack."

"Let me make this point
inadequately clear."

"I have support for
my bill from both
sides of the circle."

"I have no plans and no plans to have plans."

– *Former New York Governor Mario Cuomo, November 12, 1990*

"Schools start in August when people should be working."

"The people in my district do not want this highway bypass, no matter if it goes through or around the city."

"Our debates have been like the
mating of pandas in the zoo –
the expectations are high,
there's a lot of fuss and commotion,
but there's never any kind of result."

*– Presidential candidate and former
Governor Bruce Babbitt in 1988*

"The poorhouse is vanishing from among us. ...we shall soon...be in sight of the day when poverty will be banished from this nation."

– Herbert Hoover, 1928

"So here is the Great Society. It's the time – and it's going to be soon – when nobody in this country is poor."

– Lyndon B. Johnson, 1965

"If I give a little
and you give a lot,
we'll have a compromise."

"Good communication
is essential –
even if it isn't clear."

"I'm in favor of letting the status quo stay as it is."

"It's time to take the bull
by the tail and look her
in the eye."

"Family planning has
many misconceptions."

"We're gathering bushels
of fog on this issue."

"This proposal will use
an existing code
that already exists."

"Okay, we've won.
What do we do now?"

*– Prime Minister
Brian Mulroney, Canada*

"I know what I believe
is different from what
I know are the facts."

"This body is throwing
up this issue."

"Don't confuse me
with the facts.
I've got a closed mind."

*– Congressman
Earl Landgrebe, Indiana*

"Asking Senator Fulbright's advice on foreign policy is like asking the Boston Strangler to massage your neck."

– Spiro Agnew

"When things haven't gone well for you, call in a secretary or a staff man and chew him out. You will sleep better and they will appreciate the attention."

– President
Lyndon B. Johnson

"You can lead a dead
horse to water but you
can't make it drink."

– Mayor
Allan Lamport, Toronto

"Just destroy all the tapes."

– Richard Nixon, reflecting on lessons learned from Watergate

"My knowledge
is no match
for his ignorance."

"We have a permanent plan
for the time being."

"I caught that out of
the corner of my ear."

*– State Senator
Carol Roessler, Wisconsin*

"I'm not confused,
 I'm just too busy to think."

"There is no shortage
of lawyers in Washington,
D.C. In fact, there may be
more lawyers than people."

*– U.S. Supreme Court Justice
Sandra Day O'Connor*

"We're maximizing the
quality of our mistakes."

"One of the local funeral directors even called me up to offer a special group rate."

– *Mayor J. Michael O'Connell, Saratoga Springs, New York, one of 350 city employees who received W-2 forms listing them as dead*

"I don't necessarily believe
what I think."

"Generals should never do anything
that needs to be explained to a Senate
committee...there's nothing one can
explain to a Senate committee."

– *Harry S. Truman*

"Politics are too serious a matter
to be left to politicians."

– Charles de Gaulle

"It appears to me
   the Department wants
   Car-T Blank
   on this proposal."

"It feels like I am holding
a bunch of greased pigs together."

"Congress would exempt
itself from the law of
gravity if it could."

– *Congressman
Henry Hyde, Illinois*

"The advent of these sleek coaches should provide a tremendous shot in the arm to both legs of Nevada's passenger train system."

— Senator
Howard Cannon, Nevada

"I thought I could
speak loud enough
not to be heard."

"I come from a state where
gun control is just how steady
you hold your weapon."

*– Senator
Alan Simpson, Wyoming*

"The entire insurance industry
is suffering a favorable mortality."

"Before I begin my speech,
I have something to say."

*– Ambassador
Robert Strauss*

"There comes a time
to put principle aside
and do what's right."

"Tomorrow morning we'll have an all day meeting."

"This bill goes to
the very heart
of the moral fiber
of human anatomy."

"Now we've got them
right where they want us."

"We need to pass this bill before the day before tomorrow...which is today!"

"I think Milwaukee County
is a fine city."

"If the shoe fits, take it off."

"It takes real courage to vote
against your convictions."

"Mr. President,
    before I give you the benefit
    of my remarks, I'd like to know
    what we're talking about."

"When I started talking I was for the bill, but the longer I talk the more I know I'm against it."

"I don't see why we can't have more than one monopoly."

"Don't burn your bridges
behind you. Plan ahead –
better to burn them
in front of you."

"I'm dressed to bill."

*– A lobbyist who is
also a lawyer*

"Taxation without representation is one of the founding principles of this democracy."

"If I were to take all
the people who contacted
me on this issue and
lay them end to end,
they would all point in a
different direction!"

"I can't talk anymore.
The Senate is on the floor."

"I'm a politician,
I'll always be there
when I need you."

"You've got to stop milking
that dead horse."

"I rise to be heard because
I can't stand sitting down."

"I can't believe we're going to let a majority of the people decide what's best for their state."

"I think we need to debate the issues of mental disturbances. I can give insight on that."

"I'm in favor of any kind
of activity between
condescending adults."

"If it weren't for the
   Rural Electric Associations,
   we farmers would still
   be watching television
   by candlelight."

"We're going to consider
a bill on low-flow toilets.
You'll certainly want to
sit in on that one."

"We're caught between
the dog and the fire hydrant."

"We're not up for election
this year, so it seems
we could do what's right."

"I don't know whether we need a bill on teen pregnancy because statistics show teen pregnancy drops off significantly after age 25."

"As the Reagan presidency
ends, it is time for the
Bush pregnancy to begin."

— *Governor
Tommy G. Thompson,
Wisconsin*

"Things are more like they are now than they have ever been."

– *President Gerald Ford*

"A liberal is a man with both feet planted firmly in the air."

– *Adlai Stevenson*

"People who live
in glass houses
shouldn't bowl."

"I'll speak for the man,
or against him,
whichever will do him
most good."

— *President*
Richard M. Nixon

"A politician is a statesman
who approaches every question
with an open mouth."

– *Adlai Stevenson*

"Politicians are the only
animals who can sit on
a fence and still keep
both ears to the ground."

"Politics is like roller skating.
You go partly where you
want to go and partly where
the damned things take you."

— *Former U.S. Senator
Henry Ashurst, Arizona*

"Even the utility companies
deserve adequate constipation."

"I don't have to understand
this issue – all I know
is if that guy is against it,
I'm for it."

"Property takings are okay
as long as public officials
don't know they're doing it."

"Wait a minute. I'm not sure I understand my own question."

"This is really confusing what we are doing right now."

– said in the midst of voting on an issue

"I haven't seen so many suits
in a room since my wedding."

*– said by a farmer testifying
before a tax committee*

"I wasn't sleeping –
I was stretching my eyelids."

"Mr. Speaker, we all know that
it doesn't do us a lot of good
to close the barn door
with the horse still in there."

"I oppose this bill with every flubber of my being."

"I'm not so smart and
neither are most of the people
I represent, but even we know
that this is a bad bill."

*– said by a state representative
who, not surprisingly, lost his
reelection bid*

"There are only two ways to reduce the budget deficit...we must do both.

> – *Presidential candidate*
> *Michael Dukakis, April 1987*

"There are only three ways to reduce the deficit...we must do all three."

> – *Michael Dukakis, September 1987*

"There are only four ways to reduce the federal budget deficit...we must do all four."

> – *Michael Dukakis, August 1988*

"I'm an old Navy man;
the bow is in the rear
end, isn't it?"

– *Richard Nixon*

"Sensible and responsible
women do not want to vote."

– *Grover Cleveland*

"See what happens when you let men into the Cabinet?"

– *Secretary of State
Madeleine Albright, talking about two
male associates who'd been comparing
notes about shopping for clothes*

"I would have made
a good Pope."

– *President*
  Richard M. Nixon

"We're all fuzzy on the issues. That's proven by the fact that we did get elected. The advantage of being a Presidential candidate is that you have a much broader range of issues on which to be fuzzy."

– *President Jimmy Carter*

"A zebra cannot change its spots."

– *Senator*
Al Gore, Vice-Presidential candidate,
referring to President George Bush

"During my service in the
United States Congress,
I took the initiative
in creating the Internet."

  – *Vice-President*
    Al Gore, March 1999
    (The Internet was developed
    by the Pentagon in 1969.)

"Al Gore is so boring his Secret Service code name is 'Al Gore.'"

– *Al Gore*

"A politician has to be able
to see both sides of an issue
so he can get around it."

"He reminds me of the man who
murdered both of his parents,
and then when the sentence was about
to be pronounced pleaded mercy on
the grounds he was an orphan."

– *Abraham Lincoln*

"You can lead
  the House to order
  but you can't make
  it think."

– *Governor
  William Weld, Massachusetts*

"Don't look at me in that tone of voice."

– *Thaddeus Caraway*

"When the President does it, that means that it is not illegal."

– Richard Nixon

"I always wait until a jury
has spoken before I anticipate
what they will do."

– *Attorney-General*
Janet Reno

"When a man is asked to give a speech, the first thing he has to decide is what to say."

– President
Gerald Ford

"Mr. Speaker, the Governor of the Great State of Thompson."

– Assembly Sergeant-at-Arms,
introducing Governor Tommy G.
Thompson to the Wisconsin Legislature

"I am a man of limited talents
from a small town. I don't seem
to grasp that I am President."

– *President
Warren G. Harding*

"We're going to move left
and right at the same time."

– *Governor
Jerry Brown, California*

"I have often thought that if there had been a good rap group around in those days, I might have chosen a career in music instead of politics."

– Richard Nixon

"I am in a firm but flexible
state of indecision."

– *Congressman*
Morris Udall, Arizona

"A Nixon-Agnew administration
will abolish the credibility gap
and reestablish the truth,
the whole truth, as its policy."

– Vice-Presidential candidate
Spiro Agnew

"...whenever I can,
I watch the Detroit
Tigers on the radio."

*– President
Gerald Ford*

"It is dangerous for a national candidate to say things people might remember."

– *Eugene McCarthy*

"A successful politician's
First Commandment:
'Thou shall not commit thyself.'"

"My God! What is there in this place that a man should want to get into it?"

*– President
James Garfield*

"Get the thing straight once and for all. The policeman isn't there to create disorder. The policeman is there to preserve disorder."

– Mayor
Richard J. Daley, Chicago

"I promise you a police car
on every sidewalk."

"I would not like to be
a Russian leader.
They never know when
they're being taped."

– Richard Nixon

"The hardest thing about any political campaign is how to win without proving you are unworthy of winning."

– *Adlai Stevenson*

"Politicians are the same all over.
They promise to build a bridge
even where there is no river."

– *Nikita Khrushchev*

"By 1980 we will be self-sufficient and will not need to rely on foreign enemies...uh, energy."

– *Richard Nixon*

"Nixon was the thirty-seventh
   President of the United States;
   he had been preceded by
   thirty-six others."

   – *Gerald Ford*

"Let's all take a deep breath and relax. We're wasting energy."

– Governor
Jerry Brown, California

"Since a politician never believes what he says, he is always astonished when others do."

– *Charles de Gaulle*

"No woman in my time will be Prime Minister or Chancellor or Foreign Secretary – not the top jobs. Anyway, I wouldn't want to be Prime Minister; you have to give yourself 100 per cent."

– *Margaret Thatcher, 1969*

"It would be like sticking my head in a moose."

– Mayor
Allan Lamport, Toronto

"Outside of the killings,
  Washington has one
  of the lowest crime rates
  in the country."

– *Mayor
  Marion Barry, Washington, D.C.*

CLINTONSPEAK

"I didn't inhale."

"I did not have
sexual relations
with that woman."

"Nobody's business but ours."

"That depends on
what your definition
of 'is' is."

"An admission of making false statements to government officials is an impeachable offense."

– August 8, 1974

"Look, half the time when
I see the evening news,
I wouldn't be for me either."

"They've managed to keep their unemployment low although their overall unemployment is high."

"There are always going to be people who want to be President, and some days I'd like to give it to them."

"The problem back then, you'll remember, is that documents were destroyed, tapes were missing. The White House was not cooperating. I think the contrast is so dramatic."

– Hillary Rodham Clinton,
comparing Whitewater
to Watergate

"If I want to knock
a story off the front page,
I just change my hairstyle."

– *Hillary Rodham Clinton*

Quayleisms

"I happen to be a Republican President...ah, the Vice-President."

"I believe we're on an
irreversible trend toward
more freedom and democracy –
but that could change."

"What a waste to lose one's mind.
Or not to have a mind is being
very wasteful. How true that is."

"One word sums up the responsibility of any Vice-President, and that one word is 'to be prepared.'"

"We are ready for any unforeseen event that may or may not occur."

"If we do not succeed,
then we run the risk
of failure."

"Welcome to
President Bush,
Mrs. Bush,
and my fellow
astronauts."

"The Holocaust was an obscene period
in our nation's history. I mean in this
century's history. But we all lived in this
century. I didn't live in this century."

"If you give a person a fish,
they'll fish for a day.
But if you train a person
to fish, they'll fish for
a lifetime."

"We're all capable of mistakes,
but I do not care to enlighten
you on the mistakes we may
or may not have made."

"It's wonderful to be here
in the great state of Chicago."

"I love California;
I practically grew up
in Phoenix."

"We're going to have the best-educated American people in the world."

"...the question is whether
we're going forward
to tomorrow or whether
we're going to go past –
to the back!"

"I spend a great deal of time with the President. We have a very close, personal, loyal relationship. I'm not, as they say, a potted plant in these meetings."

"I'm the Vice-President.
They know it and they know
that I know it."

"[I support efforts] to limit the terms of members of Congress, especially members of the House and members of the Senate."

"What you guys want, I'm for."

"My friends, no matter how rough the road may be, we can and we will never, never surrender to what is right."

"Desert Storm was a
stirring victory for the
forces of aggression."

"Quite frankly, teachers are the only profession that teach our children."

"We should develop anti-satellite weapons because we could not have prevailed without them in *Red Storm Rising*."

"In George Bush,
you get experience
and with me you get
– The Future."

"In the past we have tried
too much to prevent
the making of mistakes."

"Tobacco exports should be expanded aggressively because Americans are smoking less."

"I'm not so sure that I will miss Johnny Carson, but Johnny Carson will miss me."

"Most women do not want to be liberated from their essential natures as women."

"I stand by all the
misstatements that
I've made."

"I would rather have been
a professional golfer,
but my family pushed me
into politics."

"Who's going to beat me?"

"It's going to be different
for me this time around,
running for President...
I will be in control."

– January 1999

KENNEDY QUIPS

"Kissing babies
gives me asthma."

– *John F. Kennedy,
campaigning for
Congress in 1946*

"If you don't want to work
for a living, this job is
as good as any."

– Congressman
John F. Kennedy, Massachusetts

"Mothers all want their sons
to grow up to be President,
but they don't want them
to become politicians in
the process."

"When we got into office,
the thing that surprised me
most was to find that things
were just as bad as we'd
been saying the were."

"The United States has to move
very fast even to stand still."

"I can evade questions
without help;
what I need is answers."

BUSH SOUND BITES

"My dog, Millie, knows more about foreign affairs than these two bozos Clinton-Gore."

"This is supposed to be the year of the woman in the Senate. Let's see how they do. I hope a lot of them lose."

"The Congress will push me to raise taxes, and I'll say 'No.' And they'll push again, and I'll say to them, 'Read my lips. No new taxes.'"

– George Bush, Candidate for President
August 18, 1988

"It is clear to me that both the size of the deficit problem and the need for a package that can be enacted require...tax revenue increases."

– President George Bush
June 26, 1990

"…let me tell you, this gender thing is history. You're looking at a guy who sat down with Margaret Thatcher across the table and talked about serious issues."

"It has been said by some cynic, maybe it was a former President, 'If you want a friend in Washington, get a dog.' Well, we took them literally – that advice as you know. But I didn't need that because I have Barbara Bush."

"Tell me, General,
how dead is the Dead Sea?"

"I don't want to run the
risk of ruining what is
a lovely recession."

"It's no exaggeration to say the undecideds could go one way or another."

"I'm all for Lawrence Welk. Lawrence Welk is a wonderful man. He use to be, or was, or...wherever he is now, bless him."

PLAIN SPEAKING
FROM KANSAS

"I think every country
ought to have a President."

*– Bob Dole, when asked why he was
running for President*

"Before I got this honorary
  doctorate, Senator Mitchell called
  me 'Mr. Gridlock.' But with this
  degree, I will insist on being called
  'Doctor Gridlock.'"

"If you're hanging around with nothing to do and the zoo is closed, come over to the Senate. You'll get the same kind of feeling and you won't have to pay."

"You watch all those speeches being made and nothing going on at all and you think, 'Where am I? I can't believe this.' But don't worry about it. If there are not many people there, you're lucky because you can't do business without a quorum. As long as three or four people are on the floor, the country is in good hands. It's only when you have 60 to 70 in the Senate that you want to be concerned."

"Some of us are uncomfortable
taking honoraria. I am uncomfortable
taking campaign contributions.
So, I compromised; I decided
to take both."

ACCORDING TO
THE GIPPER

"The thought of being President frightens me and I do not think I want the job."

– Ronald Reagan, seven years before being elected President

"There were so many candidates on the platform that there were not enough promises to go around."

"You can tell a lot about a fellow's character by his way of eating jelly beans."

– Ronald Reagan always had a jar of jelly beans on his desk.

"My fellow Americans...I am pleased to tell you I have just signed legislation which outlaws Russia forever. The bombing begins in five minutes."

– *perhaps Ronald Reagan's biggest OOPS! What he said as a joke before his weekly radio broadcast was in fact recorded for posterity. The President, a former radio broadcaster, had assumed the mike was "off."*

"Remember the flap when I said, 'We begin bombing in five minutes'? Remember when I fell asleep during my audience with the Pope? Remember Bitburg? Boy, those were the good old days."

"They say hard work
never hurt anybody,
but I figure why take
the chance."

"We've made no progress at all…and we didn't intend to. That's the function of a national committee."

"Even though there may be some misguided critics of what we're trying to do, I think we're on the wrong path."

"As Henry VIII said to each
of his three wives,
'I won't keep you long.'"

"Politics is not a bad
profession. If you succeed,
there are many rewards.
If you disgrace yourself,
you can always write a book."

*I WOULD WELCOME YOUR FAVORITE
FUNNY POLITICAL QUOTATIONS.
IF YOU SEND THEM TO ME, I MAY USE
THEM IN THE NEXT EDITION OF
POLITICIANS SAY THE DUMBEST THINGS*

roesslerca@aol.com

Carol Roessler is a veteran politician, serving in the Wisconsin legislature since 1983. In addition to having an occasional slip of the tongue herself, Senator Roessler has gathered countless magnificent malaprops from her colleagues and other officials from Madison to Moscow. This book proves that despite the titles and wall plaques, we're all human...and sometimes...funny! Senator Roessler acknowledges that while politics is serious business, our best laughs are at ourselves.

Acknowledgments

Thanks to all of the *politicians* who unknowingly contributed to the creation of this book.

Librarians in Fond du Lac, Oshkosh, and Madison, Wisconsin, and Washington, D.C., who answered all my questions, directed me to references and resources, conducted research, and provided thoughtful professional and personal assistance.

Barry Eigen and *June Johnson,* fellow talkers and writers, who led me to Jim Taugher at CI Design.

Jim Taugher, CI Design, for his wit, wisdom, insight, design creation, and assistance in promotion of this collection; *Tammy Schmitz* for technical production and *Rodney Gile* for the illustrations.

Peter C. Stomma, my copyright attorney.

Anne Kaestner, editor and kindred spirit, who put her long-time print and broadcast journalism talents, research and expertise to work on the manuscript and her energy, enthusiasm and resources to work on the marketing and distribution of the book.

Paul Roessler, my husband, for his wise counsel, encouragement, humor, business acumen, prayers, and energetic support.

Almighty God, for humor and His guidance all along the way.

You for selecting this book. Enjoy!

- To submit one of the dumbest things you've heard politicians say for *Politicians Say The Dumbest Things Volume II*;

- To order additional copies of *Politicians Say The Dumbest Things*, check your local book/gift store or order directly from (discount prices for group purchases and multiple orders are possible):

WRIGHT STRATEGIES
P.O. Box 1614
OSHKOSH, WI 54903
Toll Free (877) 920-6889
FAX (920) 583-3999
E-MAIL roesslerca@aol.com

Carol Roessler is a member
of the Wisconsin Professional Speakers Association
and the National Speakers Association